SECRETS

OF THE HEART

SECRETS
OF THE
HEART

Meditations of

KAHLIL GIBRAN

Selected and with a Narration by Stanley Hendricks

With an Introduction by Manoocher Aryanpur

DRAWINGS BY BILL GREER

HALLMARK EDITIONS

CONTENTS

KAHLIL GIBRAN

By Manoocher Aryanpur

If a single word could describe the mysterious art of Kahlil Gibran, that word would be "simplicity." Like Jesus and Socrates, men whom he deeply admired, Gibran compresses the most meaning into the least space. "Wisdom," he wrote, "is not in words/Wisdom is meaning within words...."

Kahlil Gibran, called today "the immortal prophet of Lebanon," was born in 1883 in the picturesque village of Bsherri. There, as a child, he discovered the beauty of nature and founded his deep faith in man's natural goodness.

After those childhood years among the cedars of Lebanon he never forgave the cities of the world for imprisoning man. "Why," he asked the world, "wear you tattered robes of narrowness while the silk raiment of Nature's beauty is fashioned for you?"

When Gibran was 11 years old, he came with his family to the New World. But he could not bear the life people led in Boston in the 1890's, and despite his family's objections he returned

7

alone to Lebanon. He was barely 14 when he disembarked at Beirut to start his studies at the school *Madrasat Al-Hekmat.*

In his four-year stay in Lebanon, the young Gibran wrote his first poems in Arabic and became known as a promising artist.

After graduation, Gibran started a life of traveling that lasted until 1910. He visited Greece, Italy, and Spain, and spent several years in Paris. There he became a friend of such enduring artists as the sculptor Rodin, the composer Debussy, and the poet and playwright Maurice Maeterlink. He was not yet 30 years old.

By the time he settled in New York, Gibran had already gained the wisdom and skill to write profoundly but simply about man, love, and truth. His haunting poems and poetic prose approach the simplicity and depth of language of the great King James Bible.

In New York he produced a galaxy of outstanding works: *The Prophet, Jesus the Son of Man, The Wanderer,* and seven other books. They impress with their unique vision, lifting the mind to an exalting world of clouds and wings, of naked purity and glowing ideals.

The words "beauty" and "love" dominate Gibran's art. He believed that to stop war men must create beauty, that without beauty there could be no liberty, that beauty must be the standard by which to judge the actions of men.

And this man of beauty was also a man of love. To him, love purified of lust is the essence of true joy and salvation. Even good works, he believed, are "love made visible."

Kahlil Gibran, the devotee of simplicity, love, and beauty, was a deeply religious man, but he belonged to no particular sect. He was a mystic, and he believed in a divine source of eternally evolving life, in the essential goodness of nature, and in the equality and brotherhood of all men.

He died on April 10, 1931, then 48 years old and at the height of his powers. Many thought his tasks had been left unfinished.

But those who knew him knew better. In the decades after his death, he has become – for millions of people throughout the world–a beloved seer whose words comfort the heart. His books are available today in more than two dozen languages. His charismatic appeal still grows as new generations discover his writings.

In this specially-revised edition of Kahlil Gibran's meditations, the editor has supplied a descriptive framework, a setting, for each meditation. The settings recreate the immediacy of Gibran's message. It is, and will remain, a message of intense hope – and of promise fulfilled.

SECRETS OF THE HEART

I came to say a word and I shall say it now. But if death prevents me, it will be said by Tomorrow, for Tomorrow never leaves a secret in the book of Eternity.

I came to live in the glory of Love and the light of Beauty, which are the reflections of God.

I am here, living, and I cannot be exiled from the domain of life, for through my living word I will live in death.

I came here to be for all and with all, and what I do today in my solitude will be echoed Tomorrow by the multitude.

What I say now with one heart will be said Tomorrow by thousands of hearts.

KAHLIL GIBRAN

I

THE RETURN

He is only a memory now, for he walks no longer the high paths of earth, but his words live among us still, and they lead us back to another time, to another place:

To a storm-tossed harbor, and an expectant crowd at dockside; to a small boat buffeted by the harsh winds and battering waves.

And in the boat a man unmindful of the furor of winds and waves, a man whose face is peaceful, calm, as if he sees beyond storm and crowd to a secret haven.

And now the boat is docked and the crowd gathers, and the storm hushes as though it, too, would wait expectantly for his words. For he has returned again among us, and, at first, quietly he speaks to all:

I HAVE only human words to interpret your dreams, your desires, and your instructions.

But God has given to each of us a spirit with wings,

Wings on which to soar into the spacious firmament of Love and Freedom.

I love you, my brothers and sisters, whoever you are.

You and I are all children of one faith, for the diverse paths of religion are fingers of the loving hand of one Supreme Being, a hand extended to all offering completeness of spirit to all, eager to receive all.

My soul, living is like a courser of the night: the swifter the flight, the nearer the dawn.

You are my brothers and sisters because you are human, and we all are sons and daughters of one Holy Spirit;

We are equal and made of the same earth.

You are here as my companions along the path of light, and my aid in understanding the meaning of hidden Truth.

I love you for your Truth, derived from your knowledge. I respect it as a divine thing, for it is the deed of the spirit.

Your Truth shall meet my Truth and blend together like the fragrance of flowers and become one whole and eternal Truth, perpetuating and living in the eternity of Love and Beauty.

Humanity, which you and I together share, is a brilliant river singing its way,
And carrying with it the mountain's secrets into the heart of the sea.

Knowledge is a light, enriching the warmth of life,
And all may partake who seek it out.

Life is that which we see and experience through the spirit;
But the world around us we come to know through understanding and reason.

The spirit, which we share, is a sacred blue torch, burning and devouring the dry plants,
And growing with the storm and illuminating the faces of the goddesses.

And if we love, our love is neither from us
nor is it for us.

If we rejoice, our joy is not in us, but in Life
itself.

If we suffer, our pain lies not in our wounds,
but in the very heart of Nature.

Everything on earth lives according to the
law of Nature,

And from the law emerges the glory and joy
of liberty.

Beauty is that which attracts the soul, and that
which loves to give and not to receive.

When you meet Beauty, you feel that the
hands deep within your inner self are stretched
forth to bring it into the domain of your heart.

It is a magnificence combined of sorrow and
joy;

It is the Unseen which you see,

And the Vague which you understand,

And the Mute which you hear.

It is the Holy of Holies that begins in yourself
and ends vastly beyond any earthly imagining.

He who loves the light will be loved by the light,

For the eternal soul is never contented; it ever seeks exaltation.

Truly I say to you that thoughts have a higher dwelling place than the visible world.

II

A COUNSELOR OF MEN

Then one at the edge of the crowd spoke, one new to the city, one who had not learned the legends, saying:

"Who are you, and by what authority do you speak these words to us?"

And the one who had come that stormy day in the small boat turned to the one at the crowd's edge and spoke again:

UNLESS I BE endowed with wide knowledge, keen judgment, and great experience, how could I count myself a counselor of men?

Like you, I have been here since the beginning, and I shall be until the end of days. There is no ending to my existence,

For the human soul is but a part of a burning torch which God separated from Himself at Creation.

Thus my soul and your soul are one, and we are one with God,

And if I count myself a counselor of men, it is only because my soul, which is one with yours, has preached to me.

My soul preached to me and taught me to love that which the evil abhor and befriend those whom they revile.

Before my soul preached to me, Love was in my heart as a tiny thread fastened between two pegs.

But now Love has become a halo whose beginning is its end, and whose end is its beginning. It surrounds every being and extends slowly to embrace all that shall be.

My soul advised me and taught me to perceive the hidden beauty of the skin, figure, and hue.

She instructed me to meditate upon that which the evil call ugly until its true charm and delight appear.

Before my soul counseled me, I saw Beauty as a trembling torch between columns of smoke.

Now, since the smoke has vanished, I see only the flame.

My soul preached to me and taught me to listen to the voices which the tongue and the larynx and the lips do not utter.

Before my soul preached to me, I heard only clamor and wailing.

But now I eagerly attend Silence and hear its choirs singing the hymns of the ages and the songs of the firmament announcing the secrets of the Unseen.

My soul preached to me and instructed me to drink the wine that cannot be pressed and cannot be poured from cups.

Before my soul preached to me, my thirst was like a dim spark hidden under the ashes that can be extinguished by a swallow of water.

But now my longing has become my cup, my affections my wine, and my loneliness my intoxication; yet, in this unquenchable thirst there is eternal joy.

My soul preached to me and taught me to touch that which has not become incarnate; my soul revealed to me that whatever we touch is part of our desire.

But now my fingers have turned into mist penetrating that which is seen in the universe and mingling with the Unseen.

My soul instructed me to inhale the scent that no myrtle or incense emits.

Before my soul preached to me, I craved the scent of perfume in the gardens or in flasks or in censers.

But now I can savor the incense that is not burnt for offering or sacrifice. And I fill my heart with a fragrance that has never been wafted by the frolicsome breeze of space.

My soul preached to me and taught me to say, "I am ready" when the Unknown and Danger call on me.

Before my soul preached to me, I answered no voice save the voice of the crier whom I know, and walked not save upon the easy and smooth path.

Now the Unknown has become a steed that I can mount in order to reach the Unknown; and the plain has turned into a ladder on whose steps I climb to the summit.

My soul spoke to me and said, "Do not measure Time by saying, 'There was yesterday, and there shall be tomorrow.'"

And before my soul spoke to me, I imagined the Past as an epoch that never returned, and the Future as one that could never be reached.

Now I realize that the present moment contains all time and within it is all that can be hoped for, done and realized.

My soul preached to me exhorting me not to limit space by saying, "Here, there, and yonder."

Before my soul preached to me, I felt that wherever I walked was far from any other space.

Now I realize that wherever I am contains all places; and the distance that I walk embraces all distances.

My soul preached to me and said, "Do not be delighted because of praise, and do not be distressed because of blame."

Before my soul counseled me, I doubted the worth of my work.

Now I realize that the trees blossom in Spring and bear fruit in Summer without seeking praise; and they drop their leaves in Autumn and become naked in Winter without fearing blame.

My soul preached to me and showed me that I am neither more than the pygmy, nor less than the giant.

Before my soul preached to me, I looked

upon humanity as two men: one weak, whom I pitied, and the other strong, whom I followed or resisted in defiance.

But now I have learned that I was as both are and made from the same elements. My origin is their origin, my conscience is their conscience, my contention is their contention, and my pilgrimage is their pilgrimage.

If they sin, I am also a sinner. If they do well, I take pride in their well-doing. If they rise, I rise with them. If they stay inert, I share their slothfulness.

My soul spoke to me and said, "The lantern which you carry is not yours,

"And the song that you sing was not composed within your heart,

"For even if you bear the light, you are not the light,

"And even if you are a lute fastened with strings, you are not the lute player."

My soul preached to me and taught me much.

And your soul has preached and taught as much to you,

For you and I are one.

❧ III ❧

ON LOVE

Then he led them away from the harbor, away from the sea, up into the hillside above the city. The way was long and arduous, but none complained, and all walked in silence, following him.

Many had questions to ask of him.

And when they were settled at his feet beneath a broad and comforting tree, a young girl shyly came forward, and in a hushed voice asked him,

"What is Love, that I have heard spoken of, but have not understood as I watched the young couples pass and the old couples sit together in their houses?"

And he gazed upon the young girl, seeing her innocence, and he said tenderly:

LOVE is the lover's eyes, and the spirit's wine, and the heart's nourishment.

Love is a rose. Its heart opens at dawn and the virgin kisses the blossom and places it upon her breast.

Love is the house of true fortune, and the origin of pleasure, and the beginning of peace and tranquility.

Love is the gentle smile upon the lips of beauty. When youth overtakes love he forgets his toil, and his whole life becomes a reality of sweet dreams.

Love is the poet's elation, and the artist's revelation, and the musician's inspiration.

Love is the sacred shrine in the heart of a child, adored by a merciful mother.

Love appears to a heart's cry and shuns a demand; love's fullness pursues the heart's desire; it shuns the empty claim of the voice. Love appeared to Adam through Eve and exile was his lot;

Yet it revealed itself to Solomon, and He drew wisdom from its presence.

Life without Love is like a tree without blossom and fruit. And Love without Beauty is like flowers without scent and fruits without seeds.

Love is like the ages – building today and destroying tomorrow;
Love is like a god, who creates ruins;
Love is sweeter than a violet's sigh;
Love is more violent than a raging tempest.

Gifts alone do not entice love; parting does not discourage love; poverty does not chase love; jealousy does not prove its awareness; madness does not evidence its presence.

Oh seekers, Love is Truth, beseeching Truth, and your Truth in seeking and receiving and protecting Love shall determine its behaviour.

❧ IV ❧

ON THE WAY OF MARRIAGE

*And now standing before him were a young man and
a young woman, their hands entwined,*
    *And they said, "Speak to us of the Way of Mar-
riage."*
    And he spoke thus:

MARRIAGE begins with the first look and the
first kiss.

The first look between lover and beloved
divides the intoxication of Life from the awakening.

It is the first flame that lights up the inner domain of the heart.

It is the first magic note plucked on the silver
string of the heart.

It is that brief moment which unfolds before
the soul the chronicles of time, and reveals to the
eyes the deeds of the night and the works of
conscience.

It opens Eternity's secrets of the future.

The first glance from the eyes of the beloved is like the spirit that moved upon the face of the waters, giving birth to heaven and earth,

When the Lord spoke and said, "Let there be."

The first kiss between lover and beloved is the first sip from the cup filled by the goddess with the nectar of Life.

It is the dividing line between Doubt that beguiles the spirit and saddens the heart,

And Certitude that floods the inner self with joy.

It is the beginning of the song of Life and the first act in the drama of the Ideal Man.

It is the bond that unites the strangeness of the past with the brightness of the future; the link between the silence of the feelings and their song.

It is a word uttered by four lips proclaiming the heart a throne, Love a king, and fidelity a crown.

It is the beginning of that magic vibration that carries the lovers from the world of weights and measures into the world of dreams and revelations.

As the first glance is like a seed sown by the goddess in the field of the human heart,

So the first kiss is the first flower at the tip of the branch of the Tree of Life.

In Marriage, love begins to render the prose of Life into hymns and canticles of praise, with music that is set by night to be sung in the day.

Here Love's longing draws back the veil, and illumines the recesses of the heart,

Creating a happiness that no other happiness can surpass but that of the Soul when she embraces God.

Marriage is the union of two divinities that a third might be born on earth.

It is the union of two souls in a strong love for the abolishment of separateness.

It is that higher unity which fuses the separate unities within the two spirits.

It is the golden ring in a chain whose beginning is a glance, and whose ending is Eternity.

It is the pure rain that falls from an unblemished sky to fructify and bless the fields of divine Nature.

As the first glance from the eyes of the beloved is like a seed sown in the human heart,

And the first kiss of her lips like a flower upon the branch of the Tree of Life,

So the union of two lovers in marriage is like the first fruit of the first flower of that seed.

ON REASON
AND KNOWLEDGE

Then a man in scholar's robes bowed to him and said,
"Speak to us of Reason and of Knowledge." And
he said :

WHEN REASON speaks to you, hearken to
what she says, and you shall be saved. Make good
use of her utterances, and you shall be as one
armed.

34

For the Lord has given you no better guide than Reason, no stronger arm than Reason.

When Reason speaks to your inmost self, you are proof against Desire.

For Reason is a prudent minister, a loyal guide, and a wise counselor. Reason is light in darkness, as anger is darkness amidst light.

Be wise: let Reason, not impulse, be your guide.

Yet be mindful that even if Reason be at your side, she is helpless without the aid of Knowledge.

Without her blood-sister, Knowledge, Reason is like houseless poverty; and Knowledge without Reason is like a house unguarded. And even Love, Justice, and Goodness avail little if Reason be not there too.

The learned man who has not judgment is like an unarmed soldier proceeding into battle. His wrath will poison the pure spring of the life of his community and he will be like the grain of aloes in a pitcher of pure water.

Reason and learning are like body and soul. Without the body, the soul is nothing but empty wind. Without the soul, the body is but a senseless frame.

Reason without learning is like the untilled soil, or like the human body that lacks nourishment.

Reason is not like the goods sold in the market-places – the more plentiful they are, the less they are worth.

Reason's worth waxes with her abundance. But were she sold in the market, it is only the wise man who would understand her true value.

The fool sees naught but folly; and the madman only madness.

I asked a foolish man to count the fools among us. He laughed and said, "This is too hard a thing to do, and it will take too long. Were it not better to count the wise?"

Know your own true worth, and you shall not perish. Reason is your light and your beacon of Truth. Reason is the source of Life.

God has given you Knowledge, so that by its light you may not only worship Him, but also see yourself in your weakness and strength.

Each day look into your conscience and amend

your faults; if you fail in this duty you will be untrue to the Knowledge and Reason that are within you.

Keep a watchful eye over yourself as if you were your own enemy; for you cannot learn to govern yourself, unless you first learn to govern your own passions and obey the dictates of your conscience.

I once heard a learned man say, "Every evil has its remedy, except folly. Christ healed the blind, the halt, the palsied, and the leprous. But the fool he could not cure."

Study a question from all sides, and you will be sure to discover where error has crept in.

He who tries to seize an opportunity after it has passed him by is like one who sees it approach but will not go to meet it.

God does not work evil. He gives us Reason and Learning so that we may ever be on guard against the pitfalls of error and destruction.

❧ VI ❧

ON JOY AND SORROW

And two in ragged clothes stood before him then,
hollow-cheeked, long-suffering, poor.

And one said to him, "Speak to us of banishing
sorrow, that we may understand the sources of your
joy, and practice to be joyful also."

And he said to them:

38

I WOULD NOT exchange the laughter of my heart for the fortunes of the multitude;

Nor would I be content with converting my tears, invited by my agonized self, into calm.

It is my fervent hope that my whole life on this earth will ever be tears and laughter,

Tears that purify my heart and reveal to me the secret of life and its mystery,

Laughter that brings me closer to my fellow-men.

Tears with which I join the brokenhearted,

Laughter that symbolizes joy over my very existence.

An eternal hunger for love and beauty is my desire;

I know now that those who possess riches alone are only miserable, but to my spirit the sighs of lovers are more soothing than music of the lyre.

When night comes, the flower folds its petals and slumbers with Love,

And at dawn, it opens its lips to receive the

Sun's kisses, bespeckled by quick dartings of clouds which come, but surely go.

The life of flowers is hope and fulfillment and peace; tears and laughter.

The water disappears and ascends until it turns into clouds that gather upon the hills and valleys;

And when it meets the breeze, it falls down upon the fields and joins the brook that sings its way toward the sea.

The life of clouds is a life of farewell and a life of reunion; tears and laughter.

Thus the spirit separates itself from the body and walks into the world of substance,

Passing like clouds over the valleys of sorrow and mountains of happiness until it meets the breeze of death and returns to its starting place,

The endless ocean of love and beauty which is God.

Some men would see the world with the eyes of God,

And would grasp the secrets of the hereafter by means of human thought.

But go instead into the field, and see how the

bee hovers over the sweet flowers and the eagle swoops down on its prey.

Go into your neighbor's house and see the infant child bewitched by the firelight, while the mother is busied at her tasks.

Be like the bee, and do not waste your spring days gazing on the doings of the eagle.

Be like the child rejoicing at the firelight and let the mother abide.

All that you see was, and still is, yours.

March on. Do not tarry. To go forward is to move toward perfection.

March on, and fear not the thorns or the sharp stones on Life's path.

❧ VII ❦

ON THE PERFECTION

OF MAN

And now the sun cast a red glow across the hillside from its setting.

A young mother stood, her babe asleep in her arms, and gazing first fondly at the babe, she said, "Speak to us of the Perfection of Man, of its attainment."

And he said:

42

YOU ASK ME, my sister, when man will reach perfection. Hear my answer:

Man approaches perfection when he feels that he is an infinite space and a sea without a shore,

An everlasting fire, an unquenchable light,

A calm wind or a raging tempest, a thunder-ing sky or a rainy heaven,

A singing brook or a wailing rivulet, a tree abloom in Spring, or a naked sapling in Autumn,

A rising mountain or a descending valley,

A fertile plain or a desert.

When man feels all these, he has already reached halfway to perfection.

To attain his goal he must then perceive that he is a child dependent upon his mother,

A father responsible for his family,

A youth lost in love,

An ancient wrestling against his past,

A worshipper in his temple,

A criminal in his prison,

A scholar amidst his parchments,

An ignorant soul stumbling between the dark-ness of his night and the obscurity of his day,

A nun suffering between the flowers of her faith and the thistles of her loneliness,

A poor man trapped between his bitterness and his submission,

A rich man between his greed and his conscience,

A poet between the mist of his twilight and the rays of his dawn.

He who can experience, see, and understand these things can reach perfection and become a shadow of God's Shadow.

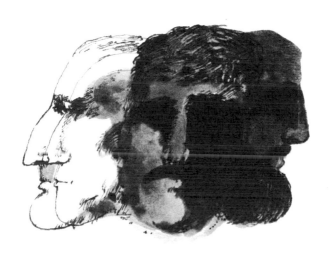

❧ VIII ❧

ON MAN'S DIVINITY

And now the sun had set, and the first star of eve-
ning appeared, and none spoke, for he had answered
many questions of them that day.

He gazed fondly upon them, upon the young and
old, upon those in rich raiment and those in rags,
upon those ill and twisted with sickness, and those
quickened with healthy life.

And he spoke then to them all in a parable, saying:

SPRING CAME, the Nature began speaking in the murmur of brooks and rivulets and in the smiles of the flowers; and the soul of Man was made happy and content.

Then suddenly Nature waxed furious and laid waste the beautiful city. And man forgot her laughter, her sweetness, and her kindness.

In one hour a frightful, blind force had destroyed what it had taken generations to build. Terrifying death seized man and beast in his claws and crushed them.

Ravaging fires consumed man and his goods; a deep and terrifying night hid the beauty of life under a shroud of ashes. The fearful elements raged and destroyed man, his habitations, and all his handiwork.

Amidst this frightful thunder of Destruction, amidst all this misery and ruin, stood the poor Soul, gazing upon all this from a distance,

And meditating sorrowfully upon the weakness of Man and the omnipotence of God.

The Soul reflected upon the enemy of Man hidden deep beneath the layers of the earth and among the atoms of the ether.

She heard the wailing of the mothers and of the hungry children and she shared their suffering.

She pondered the savagery of the elements and the smallness of Man.

And she recalled how only yesterday the children of Man had slept safely in their homes – but today they were homeless fugitives,

Bewailing their beautiful city as they gazed upon it from a distance, their hope turned to despair, their joy to sorrow, their life of peace to warfare.

The Soul suffered with the brokenhearted, who were caught in the iron claws of Sorrow, Pain, and Despair.

And as the Soul stood there pondering, suffering, doubting the justice of the Divine Law that binds all of the world's forces, she whispered into the ear of Silence:

"Behind all this creation there is eternal Wisdom that brings forth wrath and destruction, but which will yet bring forth unpredictable beauty.

"For fire, thunder, and tempests are to the Earth what hatred, envy and evil are to the human heart. While the afflicted nation was filling the firmament with groans and lamentations, Memory brought to my mind all the warnings and calamities and tragedies that have been enacted on the stage of Time.

"I saw Man, throughout history, erecting towers, palaces, cities, temples on the face of the earth; and I saw the earth turn in her fury upon them and snatch them back into her bosom.

"I saw strong men building impregnable castles and I observed artists embellishing their walls with paintings; then I saw the earth gape, open wide her mouth, and swallow all that the skillful hand and the luminous mind of genius had shaped.

"And I knew that the earth is like a beautiful bride who needs no man-made jewels to heighten her loveliness but is content with the green verdure of her fields, and the golden sands of her seashores, and the precious stones on her mountains.

"But man in his Divinity I saw standing like

a giant in the midst of Wrath and Destruction, mocking the anger of the earth and the raging of the elements.

"Like a pillar of light Man stood amidst the ruins of Babylon, Nineveh, Palmyra and Pompeii, and as he stood he sang the song of Immortality:

> Let the Earth take
> That which is hers,
> For I, Man, have no ending."

❧ IX ❧

ON THE PROMISE OF

THE FUTURE

*And at last one stood up in the midst of the crowd, a
young man, but a man of commanding presence, one
who might be a leader of the people.*

*And he said, "The day's light is gone, and we
know you cannot stay with us. But before you must
leave us, speak to us of the future. For if, as you have
said, man has no ending, what shall be our destiny?
What world may we dream of for our children, and
our children's children?"*

*And the one who had counseled them through the
day and into the evening of the day spoke then yet
once more, saying:*

FROM BEHIND the walls of the Present I can
hear the hymns of humanity.

I hear the sounds of the bells announcing the
beginning of the prayer in the temple of Beauty,

Bells molded in the metal of emotion and
poised above the holy altar – the human heart.

From behind the Future I see multitudes wor-
shipping on the bosom of Nature, their faces
turned toward the East and awaiting the inun-
dation of the morning of Truth.

I see the elders seated under the shade of cy-
press and willow trees, surrounded by youths
listening to their tales of former times.

I see the youths strumming their guitars and
piping on their reeds and the loose-tressed dam-
sels dancing under the jasmine trees.

I see the husbandmen harvesting the wheat,
and the wives gathering the sheaves and singing
mirthful songs.

I see woman adorning herself with a crown of lilies and a girdle of green leaves.

I see Friendship strengthened between man and all creatures, and clans of birds and butter-flies, confident and secure, winging toward the brooks.

I see no poverty; neither do I encounter excess. I see fraternity and equality prevailing among men.

I-see not one physician, for everyone has the means and knowledge to heal himself.

I find no priest, for conscience has become the High Priest.

Neither do I see a lawyer, for Nature has taken the place of the courts, and treaties of amity and companionship are in force.

I see that man knows that he is the corner-stone of creation,

And that he has raised himself above littleness and baseness and cast off the veil of confusion from the eyes of the soul;

This soul now reads what the clouds write on the face of heaven and what the breeze draws on the surface of the water;

Now understands the meaning of the flower's breath and the cadences of the nightingale.

From behind the wall of the Present, upon the stage of coming ages,
I see Beauty as a groom and Spirit as a bride,
And Life as a ceremony.

And when he had finished speaking, all bowed their heads,
And when they looked up again he was gone from them....
But his words they remembered, for he spoke the secrets of the heart.

THOUGHTS AND
MEDITATIONS

IN ONE ATOM are found all the elements of the earth; in one motion of the mind are found the motions of all the laws of existence; in one drop of water are found the secrets of all the endless oceans; in one aspect of *you* are found all the aspects of *existence*.

Dreams and affections are ever-living with the Eternal Spirit. They may disappear for a time, pursuing the sun when the night comes, and the stars when morning appears, but like the lights of heaven, they must surely return.

Memory alone brings naught save echoes of voices heard in the depths of long ago.

Everything on earth lives according to the law of nature, and from that law emerges the glory and joy of liberty.

The flower looks up high to see only the light, and never looks down to see its shadow. This is a wisdom which man must learn.

The eternal soul is never contented; it ever seeks exaltation.

The person who is limited in heart and thought is inclined to love that which is limited in life.

What human is able to gather in one cup the total wisdom that surrounds the world in many cups?

Be not satisfied with partial contentment, for he who engulfs the spring of life with one empty jar will depart with two full jars.

All on earth, seen and unseen, is spiritual only.

Man is empowered by God to hope and hope fervently, until that for which he is hoping takes the cloak of oblivion from his eyes, whereupon he will at last view his real self. And he who sees his real self sees the truth of real life for himself, for all humanity, and for all things.

The true light is that which emanates from within man, and reveals the secrets of the heart to the soul, making it happy and contented with life.

Truth is like the stars; it does not appear except from behind the obscurity of the night.

Truth is like all beautiful things in the world; it does not disclose its desirability except to those who first feel the influence of falsehood.

Truth is a deep kindness that teaches us to be

content in our everyday life and share with the
people the same happiness.

From a sensitive woman's heart springs the
happiness of mankind, and from the kindness of
her noble spirit comes mankind's affection.

Old age is the snow of the earth; it must,
through light and truth, give warmth to the
seeds of youth below, protecting them and ful-
filling their purpose until Spring comes and com-
pletes the growing pure life of youth with new
awakening.

We walk too slowly toward the awakening
of our spiritual elevation, and only that plane,
as endless as the firmament, is the understanding
of the beauty of existence through our affection
and love for that beauty.

For love, all of existence is an eternal shrine.

The spirit is not born to perish, but ever will
thrive and flourish.

The sea and the fog and the dew and the mist are all but one, whether clouded or clear.

How many flowers possess no fragrance from the day of their birth! How many clouds gather in the sky, barren of rain, dropping no pearls!

The seed which the ripe date contains in its heart is the secret of the palm tree from the beginning of all creation.

He who embraces the dawn of truth with his inner eyes will ever be ecstatic, like the murmuring brook.

The appearance of things changes according to the emotions, and thus we see magic and beauty in them, while the magic and beauty are really in ourselves.

It is wrong to think that love comes from long companionship and persevering courtship. Love is the offspring of spiritual affinity and unless that affinity is created in a moment, it will not be created in years or even generations.

Everything that a man does secretly in the darkness of night will be clearly revealed in daylight.

The mountains, trees, and rivers change their appearance with the vicissitudes of times and seasons, as a man changes with his experiences and emotions.

The true wealth of a nation lies not in its gold or silver but in its learning, wisdom, and in the uprightness of its sons.

Knowledge and understanding are life's faithful companions who will never prove untrue to you. For knowledge is your crown, and understanding your staff; and when they are with you, you can possess no greater treasures.

Solitude has soft, silky hands, but with strong fingers it grasps the heart and makes it ache with sorrow. Solitude is the ally of sorrow as well as a companion of spiritual exaltation.

He who does not see the angels and devils in

the beauty and malice of life will be far removed from knowledge, and his spirit will be empty of affection.

Real beauty lies in the spiritual accord that is called love which can exist between a man and a woman.

Love is the only freedom in the world because it elevates the spirit that the laws of humanity and the phenomena of nature do not alter its course.

Hearts that are united through the medium of sorrow will not be separated by the glory of happiness.

Love that is cleansed by tears will remain eternally pure and beautiful.

Every beauty and greatness in this world is created by a single thought or emotion inside a man.

The riches of the spirit beautify the face of man and give birth to sympathy and respect. The spirit in every being is made manifest in the eyes, the countenance, and in all bodily movements and gestures.

Our appearance, our words, our actions are never greater than ourselves. For the soul is our house; our eyes its windows; and our words its messengers.

He who understands you is greater kin to you than your own brother. For even your own kindred may neither understand you nor know your true worth.

Friendship with the ignorant is as foolish as arguing with a drunkard.

One just man causes the Devil greater affliction than a million blind believers.

A little knowledge that *acts* is worth infinitely more than much knowledge that is idle.

Learn the words of wisdom uttered by the wise and apply them in your own life.

Our souls are like tender flowers at the mercy of the winds of Destiny. They tremble in the morning breeze, and bend their heads under the falling dews of heaven.

Man with his understanding cannot know what the rain is saying when it falls upon the leaves of the trees or when it taps at the window panes. He cannot know what the breeze is saying to the flowers in the fields.

Printed on Hallmark Eggshell Book paper.
Composed in Bembo, a type originally cut
for the Venetian printer Aldus Manutius in
1495 by Francesco Griffo of Bologna. Ty-
pography by Saul Marks, The Plantin Press.
Designed by Harald Peter.